PLAYS BY

EDWARD ALBEE

BOX
AND
QUOTATIONS
FROM
CHAIRMAN
MAO TSE-TUNG

EDWARD ALBEE

< BOX

AND

QUOTATIONS
FROM
CHAIRMAN
MAO TSE-TUNG >

TWO INTER-RELATED PLAYS

NEW YORK 1969

ATHENEUM

Copyright © 1968, 1969 by Edward Albee
All rights reserved
Library of Congress catalog card number 69–15501
Published simultaneously in Canada by McClelland and Stewart Ltd.
Manufactured in the United States of America by H. Wolff, New York
Designed by Harry Ford
First Edition

FOR

MAEVE BRENNAN

AND

HOWARD MOSS

FIRST PERFORMED AT THE STUDIO ARENA THEATRE,
BUFFALO, NEW YORK, MARCH 6, 1968

BOX

THE VOICE OF RUTH WHITE

QUOTATIONS FROM CHAIRMAN MAO TSE-TUNG
CONRAD YAMA *as* CHAIRMAN MAO
LUCILLE PATTON *as* LONG-WINDED LADY
JENNY EGAN *as* OLD WOMAN
WILLIAM NEEDLES *as* MINISTER

Directed by ALAN SCHNEIDER

FIRST PERFORMED IN NEW YORK CITY
AT THE BILLY ROSE THEATRE, SEPTEMBER 30, 1968

BOX

THE VOICE OF RUTH WHITE

QUOTATIONS FROM CHAIRMAN MAO TSE-TUNG
WYMAN PENDLETON *as* CHAIRMAN MAO
NANCY KELLY *as* LONG-WINDED LADY
SUDIE BOND *as* OLD WOMAN
GEORGE BARTENIEFF *as* MINISTER

Directed by ALAN SCHNEIDER

INTRODUCTION

While it is true that these two short plays—*Box* and *Quotations from Chairman Mao Tse-tung*—are separate works, were conceived at different though not distant moments, stand by themselves, and can be played one without the company of the other, I feel that they are more effective performed enmeshed.

Even more . . . *Quotations from Chairman Mao Tse-tung* would most probably not have been written had not *Box* been composed beforehand, and *Mao* is, therefore, an outgrowth of and extension of the shorter play. As well, I have attempted, in these two related plays, several experiments having to do—in the main—with the application of musical form to dramatic structure, and the use of *Box* as a parenthesis around *Mao* is part of that experiment.

I may as well insist right now that these two plays are quite simple. By that I mean that while technically they are fairly complex and they do demand from an audience quite close attention, their content can be apprehended without much difficulty. All that one need do is—quite simply—relax and let the plays happen. That, and be willing to approach the dramatic experience without a preconception of what the nature of the dramatic experience should be.

I recall that when a play of mine called *Tiny Alice* opened in New York City a few years ago the majority of the critics wrote in their reviews—such as they were—that the play was far too complicated and obscure for the audience to understand. Leaving to one side the thoughts one might have about the assumption on the part of the critics that what they found confusing would necessarily confound an audience, this reportage had a most curious effect on the audiences that viewed the play. At the preview performances of *Tiny Alice* the audiences—while hardly to a man sympathetic to the play—found it quite clear; while later—after the critics had spoken on it—the audiences were very confused. The play had not changed one whit; a label had merely been attached to it, and what was experienced was the label and not the nature of the goods.

A playwright—unless he is creating escapist romances (an honorable occupation, of course)—has two obligations: first, to make some statement about the condition of "man" (as it is put) and, second, to make some statement about the nature of the art form with which he is working. In both instances he must attempt change. In the first instance—since very few serious plays are written to glorify the status quo—the playwright must try to alter his society; in the second instance—since art must move, or wither—the playwright must try to alter the forms within which his precursors have had to work. And I believe that an audience has an obligation to be interested in and sympathetic to these aims—certainly to the second of them. Therefore, an audience has an obligation (to itself, to the art form in which it is participating, and even to the playwright) to be willing to experience a work on its own terms.

I said before that these two plays are simple (as well as complex), and they *are* simple once they are experienced relaxed and without a weighing of their methods against more familiar ones.

EDWARD ALBEE

BOX

Curtain rises in darkness. Lights go up slowly to reveal the outline of a large cube. The cube should take up almost all of a small stage opening. The side facing the audience is open, but we should see the other five sides clearly, therefore the interior of the cube should be distorted, smaller at the backstage side, for example; also, none of the sides should be exactly square in shape, but the angles of distortion should not be very great—not so great as to call attention to themselves and destroy the feeling of a cube. When the lights are fully up on the cube —quite bright light which stays constant until the final dim-out—there should be five seconds' silence.

VOICE
(The VOICE *should not come from the stage, but should seem to be coming from nearby the spectator—from the back or the sides of the theater. The* VOICE *of a woman; not young, but not ancient, either: fiftyish. Neither a sharp, crone's voice, but not refined. A Middle Western farm woman's voice would be best.*

Matter-of-fact; announcement of a subject)
Box.

(Five-second silence)

Box.

(Three-second silence)

Nicely done. Well put . . .

(Pause)

. . . together. Box.

(Three-second silence. More conversational now)

Room inside for a sedia d'ondalo, which, in English—for that is Italian—would be, is, rocking chair. Room to rock. *And* room to move about in . . . some. Enough.

(Three-second silence)

Carpentry is among the arts going out . . . or crafts, if you're of a nonclassical disposition. There are others: other arts which have gone down to craft and which are going further . . . walls, brick walls, music . . .

(Pause)

. . . the making of good bread if you won't laugh; living. Many arts: all craft now . . . and going further. But *this* is solid, perfect joins . . . good work. Knock and there's no give—no give of sound, I mean. A thud; no hollow. Oh, very good work; fine timber, and so fastidious, like when they shined the bottoms of the shoes . . . *and* the instep. Not only where you might *expect* they'd shine the bottoms if they *did* . . . but even the instep.

(Two-second silence. Grudging, but not very)

And other crafts have come up . . . if not to replace, then . . . occupy.

(Tiny laugh)

4

Nature abhors, among so many, so much else . . .
amongst so much, us, itself, they say, vacuum.
                    (Five-second silence. A listing)
System as conclusion, in the sense of method as an end,
the dice so big you can hardly throw them any more.
                    (Some awe, some sadness)
Seven hundred million babies dead in the time it takes,
took, to knead the dough to make a proper loaf. Well,
little wonder so many . . . went . . . cut off, said no
instead of hanging on.
                    (Three-second silence)
Apathy, I think.
                    (Five-second silence)
Inevitability. And progress is merely a direction, move-
ment.
                    (Earnest)
When it was *simple* . . .
                    (Light, self-mocking laugh)
Ah, well, yes, when it was simple.
                    (Three-second silence. Wistful)
Beautiful, beautiful box.
                    (Three-second silence)
And room enough to walk around in, take a turn.
                    (Tiny pause)
If only they had *told* us! Clearly! When it was clear that
we were not only corrupt—for there is nothing that is
not, or little—but corrupt to the selfishness, to the cor-
ruption that we should die to keep it . . . go under
rather than . . .

5

(Three-second silence. Sigh)

Oh, my.

(Five-second silence)

Or was it the milk? *That* may have been the moment: spilling and spilling and killing all those children to make a point. A penny or two, and a symbol at that, and I suppose the children were symbolic, too, though they died, and couldn't stop. Once it starts—gets to a certain point —the momentum is too much. But spilling milk!

(Two-second silence. Firmly felt)

Oh, shame!

(A little schoolmarmish)

The *Pope* warned us; *he* said so. There are no possessions, he said; so long as there are some with nothing we have no right to anything.

(Two-second silence)

It's the *little* things, the *small* cracks. Oh, for every pound of milk they spill you can send a check to someone, but that does not unspill. That it *can* be *done* is the crack. And if you go back to a partita . . . ahhhhh, what when it makes you cry!? Not from the beauty of it, but from solely that you cry from loss . . . so precious. When art begins to hurt . . . when art begins to hurt, it's time to look around. Yes it is.

(Three-second silence)

Yes it is.

(Three-second silence)

No longer just great beauty which takes you more to ev-

6

erything, but a reminder! And not of what *can* . . . but what *has*. Yes, when art hurts . . .

(Three-second silence)

Box.

(Two-second silence)

And room enough to move around, except like a fly. That would be *very* good!

(Rue)

Yes, but so would so much.

(Two-second silence. Schoolmarmish)

Here is the thing about tension and the tonic—the important thing.

(Pause)

The release of tension is the return to consonance; no matter how far traveled, one comes back, not circular, not to the starting point, but a . . . setting down again, and the beauty of art is order—not what is familiar, necessarily, but order . . . on its own terms.

(Two-second silence. Sigh)

So much . . . flies. A billion birds at once, black net skimming the ocean, or the Monarchs that time, that island, blown by the wind, but going straight . . . in a direction. Order!

(Two-second silence)

And six sides to bounce it all off of.

(Three-second silence. Brave start again)

When the beauty of it reminds us of *loss*. Instead of the attainable. When it tells us what we cannot have . . .

7

well, then . . . it no longer relates . . . *does* it. That is the thing about music. That is why we cannot listen any more.

(Pause)

Because we cry.

(Three-second silence)

And *if* he says, or *she* . . . why are you doing that?, and, and your only honest response is: art hurts . . .

(Little laugh)

Well.

(Five-second silence)

Look! More birds! Another . . . sky of them.

(Five-second silence)

It is not a matter of garden, or straight lines, or even . . . morality. It's only when you can't come back; when you get in some distant key; that when you say, the tonic! the tonic! and they say, what is *that?* It's *then.*

(Three-second silence)

There! More! A thousand, and one below them, moving fast in the opposite way!

(Two-second silence)

What was it used to frighten me? Bell buoys and sea gulls; the *sound* of them, at night, in a fog, when I was very young.

(A little laugh)

Before I had ever seen them, before I had heard them.

(Some wonder)

But I knew what they *were* . . . a thousand miles from

8

the sea. Land-locked, never been, and yet the sea sounds . . .

(Three-second silence. Very matter-of-fact)

Well, we can exist with *any*thing; with*out*. There's little that we need to have to go on . . . evolving. Goodness; we all died when we were thirty once. Now, much younger. Much.

(Suddenly aware of something)

But it *couldn't* have been fog, not the sea-fog. Not way back *there*. It was the memory of it, to be seen and proved later. And more! and more! they're all moving! The memory of what we have not known. And so it is with the fog, which I had never seen, yet knew it. And the resolution of a chord; no difference.

(Three-second silence)

And even that can happen here, I guess. But unprovable. Ahhhhh. That makes the difference, does it *not*. Nothing can seep here except the memory of what I'll not prove.

(Two-second silence. Sigh)

Well, we give up something for something.

(Three-second silence. Listing again; pleased)

Sturdy, light . . . interesting . . . in its way. Room enough for a sedia d'ondalo, which is the Italian of . . . or for . . . *of*, I prefer . . . The Italian of rocking chair.

(Three-second silence)

When art hurts. That is what to remember.

(Two-second silence)

9

What to look for. Then the corruption . . .

(Three-second silence)

Then the corruption is complete.

(Five-second silence. The sound of bell buoys and sea gulls begins, faintly, growing, but never very loud)

Nothing belongs.

(Three-second silence. Great sadness)

Look; more of them; a black net . . . skimming.

(Pause)

And just one . . . moving beneath . . . in the opposite way.

(Three-second silence. Very sad, supplicating)

Milk.

(Three-second silence)

Milk.

(Five-second silence. Wistful)

Box.

(Silence, except for the sound of bell buoys and sea gulls. Very slow fading of lights to black, sound of bell buoys and sea gulls fading with the light)

QUOTATIONS FROM CHAIRMAN MAO TSE-TUNG

The outline of the cube remains; the set for QUOTATIONS FROM CHAIRMAN MAO TSE-TUNG *appears within the outlines of the cube during the brief blackout.*

CHARACTERS

CHAIRMAN MAO

Should be played, ideally, by an Oriental actor who resembles Mao. However, the role can be played either with makeup or a face mask. In any event, an attempt should be made to make the actor resemble Mao as much as possible. Mao speaks rather like a teacher. He does not raise his voice; he is not given to histrionics. His tone is always reasonable, sometimes a little sad; occasionally a half-smile will appear. He may wander about the set a little, but, for the most part, he should keep his place by the railing. Mao always speaks to the audience. He is aware of the other characters, but he must never look at them or suggest in any way that anything they say is affecting his words. When I say that Mao always addresses the audience I do not mean that he must look them in the eye constantly. Once he has made it clear that he is addressing them he may keep that intention clear in any way he likes—looking away, speaking to only one person, whatever.

LONG-WINDED LADY

A lady of sixty. I care very little about how she looks so long as she looks very average and upper middle-class. Nothing exotic; nothing strange. She should, I think, stay pretty much to her deck chair. She never speaks to the audience. Sometimes she is clearly speaking to the Minister; more often she is speaking both for his benefit and her own. She can withdraw entirely into self from time to time. She uses the Minister as a sounding board.

OLD WOMAN

Shabby, poor, without being so in a comedy sense. She has a bag with her. An orange; an apple, one or two cans: beans, canned meat. She will eat from these occasionally. Her bag also contains a fork, or a spoon, a napkin, and a can-opener. She is aware of everybody, but speaks only to the audience. Her reading of her poem can have some emotion to it, though never too much. It should be made clear, though, that while the subject of her speeches is dear to her heart, a close matter, she is reciting a poem. She may look at the other characters from time to time, but what she says must never seem to come from what any of the others has said. She might nod in agreement with Mao now and again, or shake her head over the plight of the Long-Winded Lady. She should stay in one place, up on something.

MINISTER

Has no lines, and stays in his deck chair. He must try to pay close attention to the Long-Winded Lady, though— nod, shake his head, cluck, put an arm tentatively out, etc. He must also keep busy with his pipe and pouch and matches. He should doze off from time to time. He must

14

never *make the audience feel he is looking at them or is
aware of them. Also, he is not aware of either Mao or the
Old Woman. He is seventy or so, has white or gray hair,
a clerical collar. A florid face would be nice. If a thin actor is playing the role, however, then make the face sort
of gray-yellow-white.*

GENERAL COMMENTS

For this play to work according to my intention, careful
attention must be paid to what I have written about the
characters: to whom they speak; to whom they may and
may not react; how they speak; how they move or do not.
Alteration from the patterns I have set may be interesting, but I fear they will destroy the attempt of the experiment: musical structure—form and counterpoint.
Primarily the characters must seem interested in what
they themselves are doing and saying. While the lines
must not be read metronome-exact, I feel that a certain
set rhythm will come about, quite of itself. No one rushes
in on the end of anyone else's speech; no one waits too
long. I have indicated, quite precisely, within the speeches
of the Long-Winded Lady, by means of commas, peri-
ods, semi-colons, colons, dashes and dots (as well as
parenthetical stage directions), the speech rhythms.
Please observe them carefully, for they were not thrown

in, like herbs on a salad, to be mixed about. I have under-
lined words I want stressed. I have capitalized for loud-
ness, and used exclamation points for emphasis. There
are one or two seeming questions that I have left the
question mark off of. This was done on purpose, as an
out-loud reading will make self-evident.

The deck of an ocean liner. Bright daylight, that partic-
ular kind of brightness that is possible only in mid-ocean.

CHAIRMAN MAO

There is an ancient Chinese fable called "The foolish old man who removed the mountains." It tells of an old man who lived in Northern China long, long ago, and was known as the foolish old man of the north mountains. His house faced south and beyond his doorway stood the two great peaks, Taihand and Wangwu, obstructing the way. With great determination, he led his sons in digging up these mountains, hoe in hand. Another greybeard, known as the wise old man, saw them and said derisively, "How silly of you to do this! It is quite impossible for you few to dig up those two huge mountains." The foolish old man replied, "When I die, my sons will carry on; when they die there will be my grandsons, and then their sons and grandsons, and so on to infinity. High as they are, the mountains cannot grow any higher and with every bit we dig, they will be that much lower. Why can't we clear them away?" Having refuted the wise old man's wrong view, he went on digging every day, unshaken in his conviction. God was moved by this, and he sent down two angels, who carried the mountains away on their backs. Today, two big mountains lie like a dead weight on the Chinese people. One is imperialism, the other is feudalism. The Chinese Communist Party has long made up its mind to dig them up. We must persevere

17

and work unceasingly, and we, too, will touch God's heart. Our God is none other than the masses of the Chinese people. If they stand up and dig together with us, why can't these two mountains be cleared away?

LONG-WINDED LADY

Well, I daresay it's hard to comprehend . . . I mean: *I* . . . at this remove . . . *I* find it hard to, well, not comprehend, but believe, or accept, if you will. So long ago! So much since. But there it was: Splash!

OLD WOMAN

"Over the Hill to the Poor-House."

LONG-WINDED LADY

Well, not splash, exactly, more sound than that, more of a . . .

(*Little laugh*)

no, I can't do that—imitate it: for I only *imagine* . . . what it must have sounded like to . . . an onlooker. An overseer. Not to *me*; Lord knows! Being *in* it. Or doing it, rather.

CHAIRMAN MAO

In drawing up plans, handling affairs or thinking over problems, we must proceed from the fact that China has six hundred million people, and we must never forget this fact.

OLD WOMAN

By Will Carleton.

18

LONG-WINDED LADY

No. To an onlooker it would not have been splash, but a sort of . . . different sound, and I try to imagine what it would have been like—*sounded* like—had *I* not been . . . well, so involved, if you know what I mean. And *I* was so *busy* . . . I didn't pay attention, or, if I did . . . that part of it doesn't re . . . recall itself. Retain is the, is what I started.

OLD WOMAN

"Over the Hill to the Poor-House"—a poem by Will Carleton.

CHAIRMAN MAO

Apart from their other characteristics, the outstanding thing about China's six hundred million people is that they are "poor and blank." This may seem a bad thing, but in reality it is a good thing. Poverty gives rise to the desire for change, the desire for action and the desire for revolution. On a blank sheet of paper free from any mark, the freshest and most beautiful characters can be written, the freshest and most beautiful pictures can be painted.

LONG-WINDED LADY

And so high!

OLD WOMAN

Over the hill to the poor-house—I can't quite make it clear!

Over the hill to the poor-house—it seems so horrid queer!
Many a step I've taken, a-toilin' to and fro,
But this is a sort of journey I never thought to go.

LONG-WINDED LADY

I'd never imagined it—naturally! It's not what one *would*.
The *echo* of a sound, or the remembering of a sound
having happened. No; that's not right either. For *them*;
for the theoretical . . . onwatcher.
(Pause)
Plut! Yes!

CHAIRMAN MAO

Communism is at once a complete system of proletarian
ideology and a new social system. It is different from any
other ideological and social system, and is the most complete, progressive, revolutionary and rational system in
human history. The communist ideological and social
system alone is full of youth and vitality, sweeping the
world with the momentum of an avalanche and the force
of a thunderbolt.

LONG-WINDED LADY

Exactly: plut!

OLD WOMAN

Over the hill to the poor-house I'm trudgin' my weary
   way—
I, a woman of seventy, and only a trifle gray—

I, who am smart an' chipper, for all the years I've told,
As many another woman thats only half as old.

LONG-WINDED LADY

And then, with the wind, and the roar of the engines and
the sea . . . maybe not even that, not even . . . plut!
But, some slight sound, or . . . or the creation of one!
The invention! What is that about consequence? Oh, *you*
know! Everything has its consequence? Or, every action
a reaction; something. But maybe nothing at all, no real
sound, but the invention of one. I mean, if you see it
happening . . . the, the thing . . . landing, and the
spray, the sea parting, as it were . . . well, then . . .
one makes a sound . . . in one's mind . . . to, to cor-
respond to the sound one . . . didn't . . . hear. Yes?

CHAIRMAN MAO

Imperialism will not last long because it always does evil
things.

OLD WOMAN

"Over the Hill to the Poor-House."

CHAIRMAN MAO

It persists in grooming and supporting reactionaries in all
countries who are against the people; it has forcibly seized
many colonies and semi-colonies and many military bases,
and it threatens the peace with atomic war.

OLD WOMAN

By Will Carleton.

CHAIRMAN MAO

Thus, forced by imperialism to do so, more than ninety per cent of the people of the world are rising or will rise up in struggle against it.

OLD WOMAN

Over the hill to the poor-house I'm trudgin' my weary way—
I, a woman of seventy, and only a trifle gray.

CHAIRMAN MAO

Yet imperialism is still alive, still running amuck in Asia, Africa and Latin America. In the West, imperialism is still oppressing the people at home. This situation must change.

OLD WOMAN

I, who am smart an' chipper, for all the years I've told,
As many another woman that's only half as old.

CHAIRMAN MAO

It is the task of the people of the whole world to put an end to the aggression and oppression perpetrated by imperialism, and chiefly by U.S. imperialism.

LONG-WINDED LADY

Yes. I think so.

CHAIRMAN MAO

Historically, all reactionary forces on the verge of extinction invariably conduct a last desperate struggle against the revolutionary forces, and some revolutionaries are apt to be deluded for a time by this phenomenon of outward strength but inner weakness, failing to grasp the essential fact that the enemy is nearing extinction while they themselves are approaching victory.

LONG-WINDED LADY

I remember once when I broke my finger, or my thumb, and I was very little, and they said, you've broken your thumb, look, you've broken your thumb, and there wasn't any pain . . . not *yet*; not for that first moment, just . . . just an absence of sensation—an interesting lack of anything.

OLD WOMAN

"Over the Hill to the Poor-House."

LONG-WINDED LADY

When they said it again, look, you've broken your thumb, not only did I scream, as if some knife had ripped my leg down, from hip to ankle, all through the sinews, laying bare the bone . . . not only did I scream as only children can—adults do it differently: there's an animal protest there, a revenge, something . . . something other—not

23

only did I scream, but I manufactured the pain. Right then! Before the hurt could have come through, I made it happen.

(Pause)

Well; we do that.

OLD WOMAN

What is the use of heapin' on me a pauper's shame?
Am I lazy or crazy? am I blind or lame?
True, I am not so supple, nor yet so awful stout;
But charity ain't no favor, if one can live without.

LONG-WINDED LADY

Yes; we do that: we make it happen a little before it need.

(Pause)

And so it might have been with someone watching—and maybe even to those who were. Who were watching. And there were, or I'd not be here.

(Pause)

I daresay.

(Pause)

The sound manufactured. Lord knows, if *I* had been among the . . . non-participators I should have done it, too; no doubt. Plup! Plut! Whichever. I'm sure *I* should have . . . if I'd seen it all the *way*, now. I mean, if I'd caught just the final instant, without time to relate the event to its environment—the thing happening to the thing happened *to* . . . then I doubt I would have. Nor would anyone . . . or most.

CHAIRMAN MAO

The imperialists and their running dogs, the Chinese reactionaries, will not resign themselves to defeat in this land of China.

OLD WOMAN

What is the use of heapin' on me a pauper's shame?
Am I lazy or crazy? Am I blind or lame?

CHAIRMAN MAO

All this we must take fully into account.

LONG-WINDED LADY

But just imagine what it must have been like . . . to be one of the . . . watchers! How . . . well, is marvelous the proper word, I wonder? Yes, I suspect. I mean, how often? ! It's not too common an occurrence, to have it . . . plummet by! One is standing there, admiring, or faintly sick, or just plain throwing up, but how often is one *there. Ever!* Well, inveterates; yes; but for the casual crosser . . . not too often, and one would have to be exactly in place, at exactly the proper time, and alert! Very alert in . . . by nature, and able to relate what one sees to what is happening. Oh, I remember the time the taxi went berserk and killed those people!

CHAIRMAN MAO

Riding roughshod everywhere, U.S. imperialism has made itself the enemy of the people of the world and has increasingly isolated itself. Those who refuse to be enslaved will never be cowed by the atom bombs and hydrogen bombs in the hands of the U.S. imperialists. The raging tide of the people of the world against the U.S. aggressors is irresistible. Their struggle against U.S. imperialism and its lackeys will assuredly win still greater victories.

LONG-WINDED LADY

Well, it didn't go berserk, of course, for it *is* a machine: a taxi. Nor did the driver . . . go berserk. Out of control, though! The driver lost and out of control it went! *Up* on the sidewalk, bowling them down like whatchama-callems, then crash!, into the store front, the splash of glass and then on fire. How many dead? Ten? Twelve? And I had just come out with the crullers.

OLD WOMAN

I am ready and willin' an' anxious any day
To work for a decent livin', an' pay my honest way;
For I can earn my victuals, an' more too, I'll be bound,
If anybody is willin' to only have me 'round.

LONG-WINDED LADY

The bag of crullers, and a smile on my face for everyone liked them so, and there it was! Careen . . . and dying . . . and all that glass. And I remember thinking: it's a movie! They're shooting some scenes right here on the street.

(Pause)

26

They weren't, of course. It was real death, and real glass, and the fire, and the . . . people crying, and the crowds, and the smoke. Oh, it was real enough, but it took me time to know it. The mind does that.

CHAIRMAN MAO

If the U.S. monopoly capitalist groups persist in pushing their policies of aggression and war, the day is bound to come when they will be hanged by the people of the whole world. The same fate awaits the accomplices of the United States.

OLD WOMAN

I am ready and willin' an' anxious any day
To work for a decent livin', an' pay my honest way;
For I can earn my victuals, an' more too, I'll be bound,
If anybody is willin' to only have me 'round.

LONG-WINDED LADY

They're making a movie! What a nice conclusion, coming out with the crullers, still hot, with a separate little bag for the powdered sugar, of course it's a movie! One doesn't come out like that to carnage! Dead people and the wounded; glass all over and . . . confusion. One . . . concludes things—and if those things and what is really there don't . . . are not the *same* . . . well! . . . it would usually be better if it were so. The mind does that: it helps.

27

CHAIRMAN MAO

To achieve a lasting world peace, we must further develop our friendship and cooperation with the fraternal countries in the socialist camp and strengthen our solidarity with all peace-loving countries.

LONG-WINDED LADY

The mind does that.

CHAIRMAN MAO

We must endeavor to establish normal diplomatic relations, on the basis of mutual respect for territorial integrity and sovereignty and of equality and mutual benefit, with all countries willing to live together with us in peace.

LONG-WINDED LADY

It helps.

CHAIRMAN MAO

We must give active support to the national independence and liberation movement in Asia, Africa, and Latin America as well as to the peace movement and to just struggles in all the countries of the world.

VOICE, FROM BOX

Box.

LONG-WINDED LADY

So; if one happened to be there, by the rail, and not too

discomfited, not in the sense of utterly defeated—though that would be more than enough—but in the sense of confused, or preoccupied, if one were not too preoccupied, and plummet! it went by! one, the mind, might be able to take it in, say: ah! there! there she goes!—or he; and manufacture the appropriate sound. But only then. And how many are expecting it!? Well, *I* am. *Now.* There isn't a rail I stand by, especially in full sun—my conditioning—that I'm not . . . already shuddering . . . *and* ready to manufacture the sound.

        (Little laugh)

Though not the sound *I* knew, for I was hardly thinking —a bit busy—but the sound I imagine someone else would have manufactured had *he* been there when I . . . WOOOOSSSH!! PLUT!!

        (Little laugh)

        VOICE, FROM BOX

Box.

        OLD WOMAN

Once I was young an' han'some—I was, upon my soul—
Once my cheeks was roses, my eyes as black as coal;
And I can't remember, in them days, of hearin' people say,
For any kind of a reason, that I was in their way!

        LONG-WINDED LADY

You never know until it's happened to you.

        29

VOICE, FROM BOX

Many arts: all craft now . . . and going further.

CHAIRMAN MAO

Our country and all the other socialist countries want peace; so do the peoples of all the countries of the world. The only ones who crave war and do not want peace are certain monopoly capitalist groups in a handful of imperialist countries which depend on aggression for their profits.

LONG-WINDED LADY

Do you.

VOICE, FROM BOX

Box.

CHAIRMAN MAO

Who are our enemies? Who are our friends?

LONG-WINDED LADY

Do you.

CHAIRMAN MAO

Our enemies are all those in league with imperialism; our closest friends are the entire semi-proletariat and petty bourgeoisie. As for the vacillating middle bourgeoisie, their right wing may become our enemy and their left wing may become our friend.

LONG-WINDED LADY

Falling! My goodness. What was it when one was little? That when you fell when you were dreaming you always woke up before you landed, or else you wouldn't and you'd be dead. That was it, I think. And I never wondered why, I merely took it for . . . well, I *accepted* it. And, of course, I kept trying to dream of falling after I'd heard it . . . tried so hard! . . . and *couldn't*, naturally. Well, if we control the unconscious, we're either mad, or . . . dull-witted.

OLD WOMAN

Once I was young an' han'some—I was, upon my soul.

LONG-WINDED LADY

I think I dreamt of falling again, though, but after I'd stopped trying to, but I don't think I landed. Not like what I've been telling you, though that was more seaing than landing, you might say . . . if you like a pun. Once, though! Once, I dreamt of falling straight up . . . or out, all in reverse, like the projector running backwards, what they used to do, for fun, in the shorts.

(Some wonder)

Falling . . . *up!*

CHAIRMAN MAO

In the final analysis, national struggle is a matter of class struggle. Among the whites in the United States it is only the reactionary ruling circles who oppress the black people.

LONG-WINDED LADY

Falling . . . *up!*

CHAIRMAN MAO

They can in no way represent the workers, farmers, revolutionary intellectuals and other enlightened persons who comprise the overwhelming majority of the white people.

VOICE, FROM BOX

Seven hundred million babies dead in half the time it takes, took, to knead the dough to make a proper loaf. Well, little wonder so many . . .

LONG-WINDED LADY

Not rising, you understand: a definite . . . falling, but . . . up!

OLD WOMAN

'Tain't no use of boastin', or talkin' over free,
But many a house an' home was open then to me;
Many a han'some offer I had from likely men,
And nobody ever hinted that I was a burden then!

LONG-WINDED LADY

Did I call them crullers? Well, I should *not* have; for

they were not even doughnuts, but the centers . . . hearts is what they called them: the center dough pinched out, or cut with a cutter and done like the rest, but solid, the size of a bantam egg, but round. Oh, they were good, and crisp, and all like air inside; hot, and you'd dip them in the confectioner's sugar. One could be quite a pig; everyone was; they were so good! You find them here and about still. Some, but not often.

OLD WOMAN

"Over the Hill to the Poor-House."

CHAIRMAN MAO

All reactionaries are paper tigers. In appearance, the reactionaries are terrifying, but in reality they are not so powerful. From a long-term point of view, it is not the reactionaries but the people who are really powerful.

VOICE, FROM BOX

Apathy, I think.

LONG-WINDED LADY

My husband used to say, don't leave her next to anything precipitous; there's bound to be a do; something will drop, or fall, her purse, her*self*. And, so, he had people be careful of me. Not that I'm fond of heights. I'm not unfriendly toward them—all that falling—but I have no . . . great affection.

(Little pause)

Depths even less.

OLD WOMAN

By Will Carleton.

CHAIRMAN MAO

I have said that all the reputedly powerful reactionaries are merely paper tigers. The reason is that they are divorced from the people. Look! Was not Hitler a paper tiger? Was Hitler not overthrown? I also said that the czar of Russia, the emperor of China and Japanese imperialism were all paper tigers. As we know, they were all overthrown.

LONG-WINDED LADY

All that falling.

CHAIRMAN MAO

U.S. imperialism has not yet been overthrown and it has the atom bomb. I believe it also will be overthrown. It, too, is a paper tiger.

LONG-WINDED LADY

And it became something of a joke, I suppose . . . I suppose. Where is she? Watch her! Don't let her near the edge! She'll occasion a do!

OLD WOMAN

And when to John I was married, sure he was good and smart,

34

But he and all the neighbors would own I done my part;
For life was all before me, an' I was young an' strong,
And I worked my best an' smartest in tryin' to get along.

LONG-WINDED LADY

He was a small man—my husband, almost a miniature
. . . not that I'm much of a giraffe. Small . . . and precise . . . and contained . . . quiet strength. The large
emotions . . . *yes*, without them, what?—all there, and
full size, full scope, but when they came, not a . . . spattering, but a single shaft, a careful aim. No waste, as in-
tense as anyone, but precise. Some people said he was
cold; or cruel. But he was merely accurate. Big people
ooze, and scatter, and knock over things nearby. They
give the impression—the illusion—of openness, of spaces
through which things pass—excuses, bypassings. But
small, and precise, and accurate don't . . . doesn't allow for that . . . for that *impression*. He wasn't cruel at
all.

CHAIRMAN MAO

The socialist system will eventually replace the capitalist
system; this is an objective law independent of man's
will. However much the reactionaries try to hold back
the wheel of history, sooner or later revolution will take
place and will inevitably triumph.

OLD WOMAN

Over the hill to the poor-house—I can't quite make it
clear.

LONG-WINDED LADY
Or cold. Neat; accurate; precise. In everything. All our marriage. Except dying. Except that . . . dreadful death.

CHAIRMAN MAO
The imperialists and domestic reactionaries will certainly not take their defeat lying down and they will struggle to the last ditch. This is inevitable and beyond all doubt, and under no circumstances must we relax our vigilance.

LONG-WINDED LADY
That dreadful death—all that he was not: large, random, inaccurate—in the sense of offshoots from the major objective. A spattering cancer! Spread enough and you're bound to kill *some*thing. Don't aim! Engulf! Imprecision!

VOICE, FROM BOX
When it was *simple* . . .
        (Light, self-mocking laugh)
Ah, well, yes, when it was simple.

OLD WOMAN
And so we worked together: and life was hard, but gay,
With now and then a baby to cheer us on our way;
Till we had half a dozen: an' all growed clean an' neat,
An' went to school like others, an' had enough to eat.

LONG-WINDED LADY
Don't let her near the edge!

36

CHAIRMAN MAO

Make trouble, fail, make trouble again, fail again . . . till their doom; that is the logic of the imperialists and all reactionaries the world over in dealing with the people's cause, and they will never go against this logic. This is a Marxist law.

LONG-WINDED LADY

Don't let her near the edge.

CHAIRMAN MAO

When we say "imperialism is ferocious," we mean that its nature will never change, that the imperialists will never lay down their butcher knives, that they will never become Buddhas, till their doom. Fight, fail, fight again, fail again, fight again . . . till their victory; that is the logic of the people, and they too will never go against this logic. This is another Marxist law.

LONG-WINDED LADY

But I hadn't thought I *was*. Well, yes, of course I *was* . . . but guarded . . . well guarded. Or, so I *thought*. It doesn't happen terribly often—falling . . . by indirection.

(Pause)

Does it?

OLD WOMAN

An' so we worked for the child'rn, and raised 'em every one;

37

Worked for 'em summer and winter, just as we ought
  to've done;
Only perhaps we humored 'em, which some good folks
  condemn,
But every couple's child'rn's a heap the best to them!

VOICE, FROM BOX

Oh, shame!

LONG-WINDED LADY

Not death: I didn't mean death. I meant . . . falling
off. *That* isn't done too often by indirection. *Is* it! Death!
Well, my God, of course; yes. Almost always, 'less you
take the notion of the collective . . . thing, which *must
allow* for it, take it into account: I mean, if all the rest is
part of a . . . predetermination, or something that has
already happened—in principle—well, under *those* con-
ditions *any* chaos becomes order. Any chaos at all.

VOICE, FROM BOX

Oh, shame!

CHAIRMAN MAO

Everything reactionary is the same; if you don't hit it, it
won't fall.

VOICE, FROM BOX

Oh, shame!

38

CHAIRMAN MAO

This is also like sweeping the floor; as a rule, where the broom does not reach, the dust will not vanish of itself. Nor will the enemy perish of himself. The aggressive forces of U.S. imperialism will not step down from the stage of history of their own accord.

VOICE, FROM BOX

The *Pope* warned us; *he* said so. There are no possessions, he said; so long as there are some with nothing we have no right to anything.

LONG-WINDED LADY

And the thing about boats is . . . you're burned . . . always . . . sun . . . haze . . . mist . . . deep night . . . all the spectrum down. Something. Burning.

CHAIRMAN MAO

Everything reactionary is the same; if you don't hit it, it won't fall.

LONG-WINDED LADY

I sat up one night—oh, *before* it happened, though it doesn't matter—I mean, on a deck chair, like this, well away from the . . . possibility, but I sat up, and the moon was small, as it always is, on the northern route, well out, and I *bathed* in the night, and perhaps my daughter came up from dancing, though I don't think

39

so . . . dancing down there with a man, well, young enough to be her husband.

OLD WOMAN

For life was all before me, an' I was young an' strong,
And I worked the best that I could in tryin' to get along.

LONG-WINDED LADY

Though not. Not her husband.

CHAIRMAN MAO

Classes struggle; some classes triumph, others are eliminated. Such is history, such is the history of civilization for thousands of years. To interpret history from this viewpoint is historical materialism; standing in opposition to this viewpoint is historical idealism.

LONG-WINDED LADY

Though not. Not her husband.

CHAIRMAN MAO

No political party can possibly lead a great revolutionary movement to victory unless it possesses revolutionary theory and a knowledge of history and has a profound grasp of the practical movement.

LONG-WINDED LADY

And what I mean is: the burn; sitting in the dim moon, with not the sound of the orchestra, but the *possible*

40

sound of it—therefore, I suppose, the same—the daughter, *my* daughter, and me up here, up *there*—this one?
No.—and being burned! In that—what I said—that all
seasons, all lights, all . . . well, one never returns from a
voyage the same.

VOICE, FROM BOX

It's the *little* things, the *small* cracks.

OLD WOMAN

Strange how much we think of our blessed little ones!—
I'd have died for my daughters, I'd have died for my sons;
And God he made that rule of love; but when we're old
    and gray,
I've noticed it sometimes somehow fails to work the other
    way.

LONG-WINDED LADY

His scrotum was large, and not only for a small man, I
think, as I remember back—and am I surmising my com-
parisons here, or telling you something loose about my
past?

(Shrugs)

CHAIRMAN MAO

Classes struggle; some classes triumph, others are eliminated.

LONG-WINDED LADY

What does it matter now, this late?—large, and not of

the loose type, but thick, and leather, marvelously creased and like a neat, full sack. And his penis, too; of a neat proportion; ample, but not of that size which moves us so in retrospect . . . or is supposed to. Circumcised . . . well, no, not really, but trained back, *to* it; trained; like everything; nothing surprising, but always there, and ample. Do I shock you?

VOICE, FROM **BOX**

And if you go back to a partita . . .

CHAIRMAN MAO

Such is history.

LONG-WINDED LADY

Do I *shock* you?

CHAIRMAN MAO

The commanders and fighters of the entire Chinese people's Liberation Army absolutely must not relax in the least their will to fight; any thinking that relaxes the will to fight and belittles the enemy is wrong.

LONG-WINDED LADY

That is the last I have in mind. My intention is only to remember.

OLD WOMAN

Strange how much we think of our blessed little ones!

42

CHAIRMAN MAO

I hold that it is bad as far as we are concerned if a person, a political party, an army or a school is not attacked by the enemy, for in that case it would definitely mean that we have sunk to the level of the enemy.

LONG-WINDED LADY

That is the last I have in mind.

CHAIRMAN MAO

It is good if we are attacked by the enemy, since it proves that we have drawn a clear line of demarcation between the enemy and ourselves.

LONG-WINDED LADY

And the only desperate conflict is between what we long to remember and what we need to forget. No; that is not what I meant at all. Or . . . well, yes, it may *be*; it may be on the nose.

OLD WOMAN

Strange, another thing: when our boys an' girls was grown,
And when, exceptin' Charley, they'd left us there alone;
When John he nearer an' nearer come, an' dearer seemed
    to be,
The Lord of Hosts he come one day an' took him away
    from me!

LONG-WINDED LADY

But, wouldn't you think a death would relate to a life?

43

. . . if not resemble it, *benefit* from it? Be *taught?* In *some* way? *I* would think.

OLD WOMAN

The Lord of Hosts He come one day an' took him away
from me!

CHAIRMAN MAO

Whoever sides with the revolutionary people is a revolutionary. Whoever sides with imperialism, feudalism and
bureaucrat-capitalism is a counter-revolutionary.

LONG-WINDED LADY

Be *taught?* In *some* way?

CHAIRMAN MAO

Whoever sides with the revolutionary people in words
only but acts otherwise is a revolutionary in speech.

LONG-WINDED LADY

I would think.

CHAIRMAN MAO

Whoever sides with the revolutionary people in deed as
well as in word is a revolutionary in the full sense.

VOICE, FROM BOX

And if you go back to a partita . . . ahhh, what when it
makes you cry!?

44

LONG-WINDED LADY

Savage how it can come, but, even more the preparations
for it. No, not *for* it, but the—*yes!* they *must* be preparations for it, unless we're a morbid species—that, over the
duck one day—the cold duck, with the gherkins and the
lemon slices, notched like a cog . . . and the potato
salad, warm if you're lucky, somebody suddenly says to
your husband, when were you first aware of death, and
he's only forty! God!, and he looks, and he says, without
even that flick, that instant of an eye to me, odd you
should ask me and I'm not even . . . well, I'm thirty-
nine, and I've begun, though if you'd asked me two
weeks ago, though you wouldn't have, and we saw you
then—and it was true; we had; two weeks ago; two weeks
before. Is it something that suddenly shows and happens
at once? At one moment? When we are aware of it we
show we are? My God!, he said; I hadn't thought of
dying since I was twelve, and, then again, *what,* sixteen,
what, when I wrote those sonnets, all on the boatman,
ironic, though. No! And the other man said, no: death,
not dying.

VOICE, FROM BOX

And if you go back to a partita . . . ahhhh, what when
it makes you cry!? Not from the beauty of it, but from
solely that you cry from loss . . . so precious.

OLD WOMAN

Still I was bound to struggle, an' never to cringe or fall—

Still I worked for Charley, for Charley was now my all;
And Charley was pretty good to me, with scarce a word
  or frown,
Till at last he went a-courtin', and brought a wife from
  town.

LONG-WINDED LADY

And another man there—an older man—someone my
family had known, some man we had at parties and once
I'd called Uncle, though he wasn't, some man I think my
sister had been seen to go around with . . . someone
who was around, said, God, you're young! You think of
death when you're knee-high to a knicker, and dying
when your cock gets decent for the first or second time,
and I mean *in* something, not the handy-pan, but when
you think of *dead!* And . . . he was drunk, though . . .
what!—well, my lovely husband looked at him with a
kind of glass, and he was a host then, and he said, with
a quiet and staid that I think is—well, what I have loved
him for, or what is of the substance of what I have
loved him for . . . Straight In The Eye! When I was
young I thought of death; and then, when I was older—
or what I suddenly seemed to be . . . dying . . . with
a kind of longing: Ngggggggg, with a look at me, as if
he could go on . . . and by God!, he slapped away,
and it was the first?, the only gesture I was . . . have,
been . . . even . . . momentarily . . . DON'T TALK LIKE
THAT!!

(Pause)

46

Slapped away with his eyes and said, I am suddenly dying, to which he added an it would seem, and while everybody tried to talk about death he wanted to talk about dying.

CHAIRMAN MAO

We should support whatever the enemy opposes and oppose whatever the enemy supports.

VOICE, FROM BOX

When art begins to hurt . . . when art begins to hurt, it's time to look around. Yes it is.

LONG-WINDED LADY

But, of course, my sister's . . . savior, or whatever you would have it, wouldn't not be still. *He* went *on!* Death!, he said. And then he would lapse . . . for nothing, that I could see, beyond the curious pleasure of lapsing . . . Death! Yes, my husband would say, or *said . . . said* this particular time—and Bishop Berkeley will be wrong, he added, and no one understood, which is hardly surprising—I am suddenly dying, and I want no nonsense about it! Death? You stop about death, finally, seriously, when you're on to *dying.* Oh, come on!, the other said; death is the whole thing. He drank, as . . . my sister did, too; she died. I think they got in bed together—took a bottle with them, made love perhaps. CRAP!—which quieted the room some . . . and me, too. He never did that. Death is nothing; there . . . there *is* no death.

There is only life and dying.

CHAIRMAN MAO

A revolution is not a dinner party, or writing an essay, or painting a picture, or doing embroidery; it cannot be so refined, so leisurely and gentle, so temperate, kind, courteous, restrained and magnanimous. A revolution is an insurrection, an act of violence by which one class overthrows another.

VOICE, FROM BOX

When art begins to hurt, it's time to look around. Yes it is.

LONG-WINDED LADY

And *I*, he said, *I*—thumping his chest with the flat of his hand, slow, four, five times—*I* . . . am *dying*.

CHAIRMAN MAO

After the enemies with guns have been wiped out, there will still be enemies without guns; they are bound to struggle desperately against us, and we must never regard these enemies lightly. If we do not now raise and understand the problem in this way, we shall commit the gravest mistakes.

VOICE, FROM BOX

Yes it is.

48

LONG-WINDED LADY

And I, he said, I am dying. And this was long before he did. That night he told me: I was not aware of it before. We were resting . . . *before* sex—which we would not have that night; on our sides, his chest and groin against my back and buttocks, his hand between my breasts, the sand of his chin nice against my neck. I always knew I would die—I'm not a fool, but I had no sense of time; I didn't know it would be so soon. I turned; I cupped my hands around his lovely scrotum and our breaths were together. But, it won't be for so very *long.* Yes, he said; I know. Silence, then added; but always shorter.

OLD WOMAN

And Charley was pretty good to me, with scarce a word or frown,

Till at last he went a-courtin', and brought a wife from town.

She was somewhat dressy, an' hadn't a pleasant smile.

CHAIRMAN MAO

People all over the world are now discussing whether or not a third world war will break out. On this question, too, we must be mentally prepared and do some analysis. We stand firmly for peace and against war. But if the imperialists insist on unleashing another war, we should not be afraid of it.

LONG-WINDED LADY

And I, he said, I am dying.

49

CHAIRMAN MAO

If the imperialists insist on launching a third world war,
the whole structure of imperialism will utterly collapse.

LONG-WINDED LADY

But what about *me!* Think about *me!*

OLD WOMAN

She was somewhat dressy, an' hadn't a pleasant smile—
She was quite conceity, and carried a heap o' style;
But if ever I tried to be friends, I did with her, I know;
But she was hard and proud, an' I couldn't make it go.

LONG-WINDED LADY

ME! WHAT ABOUT ME!

(Pause)

That may give the impression of selfishness, but that is
not how I intended it, nor how it is . . . at all. *I* . . .
am *left*.

(Helpless shrug)

He isn't. I'll not touch his dying again. It was long, and
coarse, and ugly, and cruel, and tested the man beyond
his . . . beyond *anyone's* capacities. I dare you! I dare
anyone! Don't scream! Don't hate! I dare anyone.

(Softer)

All that can be done is turn into a beast; the dumb
thing's agony is none the less, but it doesn't understand
why, the agony. And maybe that's enough comfort: **not**
to know why.

50

(Pause; wistful; sad)

But I am *left*.

VOICE, FROM BOX

And the beauty of art is order.

CHAIRMAN MAO

We desire peace. However, if imperialism insists on fight-
ing a war, we will have no alternative but to take the firm
resolution to fight to the finish before going ahead with
our constriction. If you are afraid of war day in day out,
what will you do if war eventually comes? First I said
that the East Wind is prevailing over the West Wind
and war will not break out, and now I have added these
explanations about the situation in case war should break
out. Both possibilities have thus been taken into account.

OLD WOMAN

She was somewhat dressy, an' hadn't a pleasant smile—
She was quite conceity, an' carried a heap o' style;
But if ever I tried to be friends, I did with her, I know.

LONG-WINDED LADY

Besides, his dying is all over; all gone, but his *death* stays.
He said death was not a concern, but he meant his own,
and for *him*. No, well, he was right: *he* only had his
dying. I have both.

(Sad chuckle)

Oh, what a treasurehouse! I can exclude his dying; I can

not think about it, except the times I want it back—the times I want, for myself, something less general than . . . tristesse. Though that is usually enough. And what for my daughter—*mine*, now, you'll notice; no longer ours; what box have I got for her? Oh . . . the ephemera: jewelry, clothes, chairs . . . and the money: enough. Nothing solid, except my dying, my death, those two, and the thought of her own. The former, though.

VOICE, FROM BOX

Not what is familiar, necessarily, but order.

CHAIRMAN MAO

War is the highest form of struggle for resolving contradictions, when they have developed to a certain stage, between classes, nations, states, or political groups, and it has existed ever since the emergence of private property and of classes.

LONG-WINDED LADY

(A little stentorian; disapproving)

Where were *you* those six last months, the time I did *not* need you, with my hands full of less each day; my arms.

(Sad, almost humorous truth)

If you send them away to save them from it, you resent their going and *they* want what they've missed. Well . . . I see as much of you as I'd like, my dear. Not as much as either of us should want, but as much as we do. Odd.

VOICE, FROM BOX

. . . and the beauty of art is order—not what is familiar, necessarily, but order . . . on its own terms.

OLD WOMAN

But she was hard and proud, an' I couldn't make it go.
She had an edication, an' that was good for her;
But when she twitted me on mine, 'twas carryin' things
    too fur;
An' I told her once, 'fore company (an' it almost made
    her sick),
That I never swallowed a grammar, or 'et a 'rithmetic.

LONG-WINDED LADY
(New subject)
And there I was! Falling!

CHAIRMAN MAO

Revolutionary war is an antitoxin which not only eliminates the enemy's poison but also purges us of our own filth.

VOICE, FROM BOX

That is the thing about music. That is why we cannot listen any more.
(Pause)
Because we cry.

LONG-WINDED LADY

We see each other less, she and I—my daughter—as I

53

said, and most often on boats: something about the air; the burning. She was with me when I fell. Well: on *board*. When they . . . hauled me in—oh, what a spectacle *that* was!—there she was, looking on. Not near where I came in, exactly, but some way off: nearer where I'd done it; where it had been done. Red hair flying—not natural, a kind of purple to it, but stunning; quite stunning—cigarette; *always*; the French one. Nails the color of blood—artery blood, darker than the vein. The things one knows! Looking on, not quite a smile, not quite not. I looked up, dolphins resting on my belly, seaweed-twined, like what's-his-name, or hers . . . I'll bet all you'll say is Honestly, Mother!

(Slight pause)

And when she came to my cabin, after the doctor, and the welcome brandy, and the sedative, the unnecessary sedative . . . there she stood for a moment, cigarette still on, in her mouth, I think. She looked for a moment. Honestly, Mother!, she said, laughing a little in her throat, *at* it, humor *at* it. Honestly, Mother! And then off she went.

VOICE, FROM BOX

That is why we cannot listen any more.

OLD WOMAN

So 'twas only a few days before the thing was done—
They was a family of themselves, and I another one;
And a very little cottage one family will do,

But I never have seen a house that was big enough for two.

VOICE, FROM BOX

Because we cry.

LONG-WINDED LADY

Where is she now. This trip. Mexico. You'd better chain yourself to the chair, she said to me, later, the day after. You *will* go on deck; put a long cord on yourself. It's not a usual occurrence, I told her; not even for me. No, but you're inventive, she said.

VOICE, FROM BOX

Look! More birds! Another . . . sky of them.

CHAIRMAN MAO

History shows that wars are divided into two kinds, just and unjust. We Communists oppose all unjust wars that impede progress, but we do not oppose progressive, just wars. Not only do we Communists not oppose just wars, we actively participate in them. All wars that are progressive are just, and all wars that impede progress are unjust. The way to oppose a war of this kind is to do everything possible to prevent it before it breaks out and, once it breaks out, to oppose war with war, to oppose unjust war with just war, whenever possible.

OLD WOMAN

But I never have seen a house that was big enough for two.

55

LONG-WINDED LADY

Mexico; still; probably. I'm in Mexico, in case you care, she said. Four A.M. First words, no hello, Mother, or sorry to wake you up if you're sleeping, if you're not lying there, face all smeared, hair in your net, bed jacket still on, propped up, lights out, wondering whether you're asleep or not. No; not that. Not even that. I'm in Mexico, in case you care.

VOICE, FROM BOX

Look! More birds! Another . . . sky of them.

LONG-WINDED LADY

Oh. Well . . . how very nice. I'm in Mexico, in case you care. I'm with two boys. Sort of defiant. Oh? Well, how nice. Add 'em up and they're just my age; one's twenty and the other's not quite that. Still defiant. Well, that's . . . she lies a bit; she's forty-two. That's very *nice*, dear. They're both Mexican. She sounded almost ugly, over the phone, in the dark. Well . . . They're both uncircumcised, she said, and then waited. When this happens . . . when this happens, she will wait—not those very words, but something she hopes to affect me with, hurt me, shock, perhaps, make me feel less . . . well, I was going to say happy, but I am seldom that: not any more . . . make me feel less even. She'll wait, and I can hear her waiting, to see if I put the phone down. If I do *not*, after a certain time, of the silence, then she *will*. I put it down gently, when I do. She slams. This time, I put it down; gently. I've never known which makes her happier . . . if either does, though I suppose one must. Whether she is happier if she makes me do it, or if I pause too long, and she can. I would like to ask her, but it is not the sort of question one can ask a forty-two-year-old woman . . . daughter or no.

VOICE, FROM BOX

It's only when you can't come back; when you get in some distant key; that when you say, the tonic! the tonic! and they say, what is *that?* It's *then.*

OLD WOMAN

An' I never could speak to suit her, never could please her
 eye,
An' it made me independent, an' then I didn't try;
But I was terribly staggered, an' felt it like a blow,
When Charley turned ag'in me, an' told me I could go!

LONG-WINDED LADY

I *do wish* sometimes . . . just in general, I mean . . . I *do wish* sometimes . . .

CHAIRMAN MAO

Some people ridicule us as advocates of the "omnipotence of war." Yes, we are advocates of the omnipotence of revolutionary war; that is good, not bad, it is Marxist.

LONG-WINDED LADY

Just in general, I mean . . . I *do wish* sometimes . . .

57

CHAIRMAN MAO

Experience in the class struggle in the era of imperialism teaches us that it is only by the power of the gun that the working class and the laboring masses can defeat the armed bourgeoisie and landlords; in this sense we may say that only with guns can the whole world be transformed.

LONG-WINDED LADY

I suppose that's why I came this time . . . the Mexicans; the boys. Put an ocean between. It's not as far as a death, but . . . still.

OLD WOMAN

"Over the Hill to the Poor-House," by Will Carleton.

LONG-WINDED LADY

I remember, I walked to the thing, the railing. To look over. Why, I don't *know:* water never changes, the Atlantic, *this* latitude. But if you've been sitting in a chair, that is what you *do:* you put down the Trollope or James or sometimes Hardy, throw off the rug, and, slightly unsteady from suddenly up from horizontal . . . you walk to the thing . . . the railing. It's that simple. You look for a bit, smell, sniff, really; you look down to make sure it's moving, and then you think shall you take a turn, and you usually do not; you go back to your rug and your book. Or *not* to your book, but to your *rug*, which you

58

pull up like covers and pretend to go to sleep. The one
thing you do *not* do is fall off the ship!

VOICE, FROM BOX

There! More! A thousand, and one below them, moving
fast in the opposite way!

OLD WOMAN

I went to live with Susan: but Susan's house was small,
And she was always a-hintin' how snug it was for us all;
And what with her husband's sisters, and what with
　child'rn three,
'Twas easy to discover that there wasn't room for me.

LONG-WINDED LADY

Here's a curious thing! Whenever I'm in an aeroplane—
which I am not, often, for I like to choose my company:
not that I'm a snob, heavens!, it's my daughter who will
not see *me*, or, rather, not often. Not that I am a snob,
but I feel that travel in rooms is so much nicer: boats and
trains, where one can get away and then out again; people are nicer when you come upon them around corners,
or opening doors. But whenever I'm up there, closed in,
strapped to my seat, with all the people around, and the
double windows, those tiny windows, and the great heavy
door, bolted from the outside, probably, even when I'm
plumped down in an inside seat—or aisle, as they call
them—*then!* It's then that I feel that I'm going to fall
out. Fall right out of the aeroplane! I don't know how I

59

could possibly do it—even through the most . . . reprehensible carelessness. I probably couldn't, even if I felt I had to. But I'm sure I will! Always! Though, naturally, I never do.

VOICE, FROM BOX
What was it used to frighten me?

CHAIRMAN MAO
Revolutions and revolutionary wars are inevitable in class society, and without them it is impossible to accomplish any leap in social development and to overthrow the reactionary ruling classes and therefore impossible for the people to win political power.

OLD WOMAN
'Twas easy to discover that there wasn't room for me.

LONG-WINDED LADY
Coarse, and ugly, and long, and cruel. That dying. My lovely husband.
(Small pause)
But I said I wouldn't dwell on that.

OLD WOMAN
An' then I went to Thomas, the oldest son I've got:
For Thomas's buildings'd cover the half of an acre lot;
But all the child'rn was on me—I couldn't stand their
   sauce—

60

And Thomas said I needn't think I was comin' there to boss.

LONG-WINDED LADY
Well! What can we say of an aging lady walks bright as you please from her rug and her Trollope or her James or sometimes her Hardy right up to the thing . . . the railing; walks right up, puts her fingers, rings and all, right on the varnished wood, sniffs . . . that air!, feels the railing, hard as wood, knows it's there—it *is* there—and suddenly, as sudden and sure as what you've always known and never quite admitted to yourself, it is *not* there; there is no railing, no wood, no metal, no buoy-life-thing saying S.S. or H.M.S. whatever, no . . . nothing! Nothing at all! The fingers are claws, and the varnish they rubbed against is air? And suddenly one is . . . well, what would you expect?! One is suddenly leaning on one's imagination—which is poor support, let me tell you . . . at least in *my* case—leaning on that, which doesn't last for long, and over one goes!

VOICE, FROM BOX
. . . a thousand miles from the sea. Land-locked, never been, and yet the sea sounds . . .

CHAIRMAN MAO
War, this monster of mutual slaughter among men, will be finally eliminated by the progress of human society, and in the not too distant future, too.

61

VOICE, FROM BOX

A thousand miles from the sea. Land-locked.

CHAIRMAN MAO

But there is only one way to eliminate it and that is to oppose war with war, to oppose counter-revolutionary war with revolutionary war, to oppose national counter-revolutionary war with national revolutionary war, and to oppose counter-revolutionary class war with revolutionary class war.

VOICE, FROM BOX

Never been, and yet the sea sounds.

CHAIRMAN MAO

When human society advances to the point where classes and states are eliminated, there will be no more wars, counter-revolutionary or revolutionary, unjust or just. That will be the era of perpetual peace for mankind.

OLD WOMAN

But all the child'rn was on me—I couldn't stand their sauce—
And Thomas said I needn't think I was comin' there to boss.

LONG-WINDED LADY

Over one goes, and it's a long way, let me tell you! No falling *up*; no, siree; or out! Straight down! As straight as anything! Plummet! Plut! Well, plummet for sure, plut conjectural. I wonder why I didn't kill myself. Exactly what my daughter said: I wonder why you didn't kill yourself. Though her reading was special. Had a note of derision to it.

OLD WOMAN
An' then I wrote to Rebecca, my girl who lives out West,
And to Isaac, not far from her—some twenty miles at best;
And one of 'em said 'twas too warm there for anyone so old,
And t'other had an opinion the climate was too cold.

VOICE, FROM BOX
Well, we give up something for something.

LONG-WINDED LADY
I did *not* kill myself, as *I* see it, through a trick of the wind, or chance, or because I am bottom heavy. Straight down like a drop of shot! Except. Except, at the very end, a sort of curving, a kind of arc, which sent me gently into a rising wave, or throw-off from the boat, angling into it just properly, sliding in so that it felt like falling on leaves —the pile of autumn leaves we would make, or our brother would, and jump on, like a feather bed. A gust of wind must have done that. Well . . . something did.

CHAIRMAN MAO
"War is the continuation of politics." In this sense war is

politics and war itself is a political action; since ancient times there has never been a war that did not have a political character. "War is the continuation of politics by other means."

VOICE, FROM BOX
Something for something.

CHAIRMAN MAO
It can therefore be said that politics is war without bloodshed while war is politics with bloodshed.

VOICE, FROM BOX
When art hurts. That is what to remember.

LONG-WINDED LADY
I try to recall if I recall the falling, but I'm never sure, I think I do, and then I think I have not. It was so like being awake and asleep . . . at the same time. But I *do* recall being in the water. Heavens! What a sight! *I* must have been, too, but I mean what I *saw:* the sliding by of the ship, green foam in the mouth—kind of exciting—green foam as the wake went by. Lucky you missed the propellers, they said afterwards. Well, yes; lucky.

CHAIRMAN MAO
Without armed struggle neither the proletariat, nor the

people, nor the Communist Party would have any standing at all in China and it would be impossible for the revolution to triumph.

OLD WOMAN

And one of 'em said 'twas too warm there for anyone so
    old,
And t'other had an opinion the climate was too cold.

LONG-WINDED LADY

And sitting there! Sitting there in the water, bouncing
around like a carton, screaming a little, not to call attention or anything like that, but because of the fright, and
the surprise, and the cold, I suppose; and . . . well . . .
because it was all sort of thrilling: watching the boat
move off. My goodness, boats move fast! Something you
don't notice till you're off one.

VOICE, FROM BOX

Then the corruption is complete.

OLD WOMAN

So they have shirked and slighted me, an' shifted me
    about—
So they have wellnigh soured me, an' wore my old heart
    out;
But still I've borne up pretty well, an' wasn't much put
    down,

Till Charley went to the poor-master, an' put me on the town.

LONG-WINDED LADY

And then . . . and then horns, and tooting, and all sorts of commotion and people running around and pointing . . .

(Some disappointment)

and then the boats out, the launches, and dragging me in and hauling me up—in front of all those people!—and then the brandy and the nurse and the sedative . . . and all the rest.

(Pause)

I lost my cashmere sweater . . . and one shoe.

CHAIRMAN MAO

We are advocates of the abolition of war; we do not want war; but war can only be abolished through war, and in order to get rid of the gun it is necessary to take up the gun.

LONG-WINDED LADY

You're a very lucky woman, I remember the chief purser saying to me, the next day; I was still groggy. You're a very lucky woman. Yes, I am, I said; yes; I am.

CHAIRMAN MAO

Every Communist must grasp the truth, "Political power grows out of the barrel of a gun."

66

VOICE, FROM BOX

Nothing belongs.

OLD WOMAN

But still I've borne up pretty well, an' wasn't much put
down,
Till Charley went to the poor-master, an' put me on the
town.

LONG-WINDED LADY

Then, of course, there were the questions. People don't
fall off of ocean liners very often. No, I don't suppose
they do. Broad daylight and all, people on deck. No; no;
I don't imagine so. Do you think you slipped? Surely not!
Dry as paint. Have you . . . do you cross often? Oh,
heavens, yes! I've done it for years. Have you . . . has
this sort of thing ever happened before? What do you
take me for!? I'm lucky I'm back from this one, I suppose. Then—gratuitously, and a little peevish, I'm afraid
—and I shall cross many times more! And I have—many
times, and it's not happened again. Well, do you . . .
do you think maybe you were—wincing some here:
them; not me—you were helped? Helped? What do you
mean? Well . . . aided. What do you mean, *pushed?*
Bedside nod. Yes. A laugh from me; a young-girl laugh:
hand to my throat, head back. Pushed! Good gracious,
no! I had been *reading.* What were you reading—which
struck me as beside the point and rather touching. Trol-

67

lope, I said, which wasn't true, for that had been the day
before, but I said it anyway.

(Some wonder)

They didn't know who Trollope was. Well, *there's* a life
for you!

OLD WOMAN

Over the hill to the poor-house—my child'rn dear,
  good-by!
Many a night I've watched you when only God was nigh;
And God'll judge between us; but I will al'ays pray
That you shall never suffer the half I do today.

VOICE, FROM BOX

Look; more of them; a black net . . . skimming.

(Pause)

And just one . . . moving beneath . . . in the opposite
way.

LONG-WINDED LADY

Isn't that *some*thing? You lead a whole life; you write
books, or you do not; you strive to do good, and succeed,
sometimes, amongst the bad—the bad never through de-
sign, but through error, or chance, or lack of a chemical
somewhere, in the head, or cowardice, maybe—you raise
a family and live with people, see them *through* it; you
write books, or you do not, and you say your name is
Trollope . . . or whatever it may be, no matter what,

68

you say your name . . . and they have . . . never . . . heard of it. That *is* a life for you.

VOICE, FROM BOX
Milk.

CHAIRMAN MAO
People of the world, unite and defeat the U.S. aggressors and all their running dogs! People of the world, be courageous, dare to fight, defy difficulties and advance wave upon wave. Then the whole world will belong to the people. Monsters of all kinds shall be destroyed.

OLD WOMAN
"Over the Hill to the Poor-House," by Will Carleton.

VOICE, FROM BOX
Milk.

LONG-WINDED LADY
Is there any chance, do you think . . . Hm? . . . I say, is there any chance, do you think, well, I don't know how to put it . . . do you think . . . do you think you may have done it on purpose? Some silence. I look at them, my gray eyes gently wide, misting a little in the edges, all innocence and hurt: *true* innocence; *true* hurt. That I may have done it on purpose? Yes; thrown yourself off.
    (Some bewilderment and hurt)
. . . Me?

CHAIRMAN MAO

People of the world, unite and defeat the U.S. aggressors
and all their running dogs.

LONG-WINDED LADY

Well; yes; I'm sorry. Thrown myself off? A clearing of
the throat. Yes. Tried to kill yourself.

(*A sad little half-laugh*)

Good heavens, no; *I* have nothing to die for.

BOX

(REPRISE)

Perhaps keep the figures from Quotations from Chairman Mao Tse-tung *still and put them in silhouette. Raise the light on the outline of the Box again.*

VOICE

If only they had *told* us! Clearly! When it was clear that we were not only corrupt—for there is nothing that is not, or little—but corrupt to the selfishness, to the corruption that we should die to keep it . . . go under rather than . . .
> (*Three-second silence. Sigh*)

Oh, my.
> (*Five-second silence*)

And if you go back to a partita . . . ahhhhh, what when it makes you cry!? Not from the beauty of it, but from solely that you cry from loss . . . so precious. When art begins to hurt . . . when art begins to hurt, it's time to look around. Yes it is.
> (*Three-second silence*)

Yes it is.
> (*Three-second silence*)

No longer just great beauty which takes you more to everything, but a reminder! And not of what *can* . . . but what *has*. Yes, when art hurts . . .

(Three-second silence)

Box.

(Two-second silence)

So much . . . flies. A billion birds at once, black net skimming the ocean, or the Monarchs that time, that island, blown by the wind, but going straight . . . in a direction. Order!

(Two-second silence)

When the beautiy of it reminds us of *loss*. Instead of the attainable. When it tells us what we cannot have . . . well, then . . . it no longer relates . . . *does* it. That is the thing about music. That is why we cannot listen any more.

(Pause)

Because we cry.

(Five-second silence)

Look! More birds! Another . . . sky of them.

(Five-second silence)

What was it used to frighten me? Bell buoys and sea gulls; the *sound* of them, at night, in a fog, when I was very young.

(A little laugh)

Before I had ever seen them, before I had heard them.

(Some wonder)

But I knew what they *were* . . . a thousand miles from

the sea. Land-locked, never been, and yet the sea sounds . . .

(Three-second silence)

But it *couldn't* have been fog, not the sea-fog. Not way back *there*. It was the memory of it, to be seen and proved later. And more! and more! they're all moving! The memory of what we have not known. And so it is with the fog, which I had never seen, yet knew it. And the resolution of a chord; no difference.

(Three-second silence)

And even that can happen here, I guess. But unprovable. Ahhhhh. That makes the difference, does it *not*. Nothing can seep here except the memory of what I'll not prove.

(Two-second silence. Sigh)

Well, we give up something for something.

(Three-second silence)

When art hurts. That is what to remember.

(Two-second silence)

What to look for. Then the corruption . . .

(Three-second silence)

Then the corruption is complete.

> *(Five-second silence. The sound of bell buoys and sea gulls begins, faintly, growing, but never very loud)*

Nothing belongs.

(Three-second silence. Great sadness)

Look; more of them; a black net . . . skimming.

73

(Pause)

And just one . . . moving beneath . . . in the opposite way.

(Three-second silence. Very sad, supplicating)

Box.

(Silence, except for the sound of bell buoys and sea gulls. Very slow fading of lights to black, sound of bell buoys and sea gulls fading with the light)

EDWARD ALBEE

Edward Albee was born in 1928, and began writing plays thirty years later. His previous plays are, in order of composition, The Zoo Story (1958); The Death of Bessie Smith (1959); The Sandbox (1959); The American Dream (1960); Who's Afraid of Virginia Woolf? (1961–1962); The Ballad of the Sad Café, *adapted from Carson McCullers' novella* (1963); Tiny Alice (1964); Malcolm, *adapted from James Purdy's novel* (1965); A Delicate Balance (1966); *and* Everything in the Garden, *adapted from the play by Giles Cooper* (1967).